IT'S TIME TO EAT JELLY BEANS

It's Time to Eat JELLY BEANS

Walter the Educator

Silent King Books
A WhichHead Entertainment Imprint

Copyright © 2024 by Walter the Educator

All rights reserved. No part of this book may be reproduced in any manner whatsoever without written per- mission except in the case of brief quotations embodied in critical articles and reviews.

First Printing, 2024

Disclaimer

This book is a literary work; the story is not about specific persons, locations, situations, and/or circumstances unless mentioned in a historical context. Any resemblance to real persons, locations, situations, and/or circumstances is coincidental. This book is for entertainment and informational purposes only. The author and publisher offer this information without warranties expressed or implied. No matter the grounds, neither the author nor the publisher will be accountable for any losses, injuries, or other damages caused by the reader's use of this book. The use of this book acknowledges an understanding and acceptance of this disclaimer.

It's Time to Eat JELLY BEANS is a collectible early learning book by Walter the Educator suitable for all ages belonging to Walter the Educator's Time to Eat Book Series. Collect more books at WaltertheEducator.com

USE THE EXTRA SPACE TO TAKE NOTES AND DOCUMENT YOUR MEMORIES

JELLY BEANS

Jelly beans, jelly beans, shiny and small,

It's Time to Eat

Jelly Beans

A rainbow of colors, let's taste them all!

Tiny and sweet, a treat so neat,

They're fun to share and even more to eat.

Red ones taste like cherries so bright,

Yellow like lemons, a sunny delight.

Green ones bring a tangy surprise,

Blue tastes like the sky with sparkling skies.

Orange is juicy, just like the fruit,

Pink tastes like candy, oh what a hoot!

Purple is grape, a flavor so sweet,

All mixed together, they're such a treat.

Shake the bag, hear the fun sound,

Pour them out and pass them around.

A handful of joy, colors so grand,

Each little bean fits right in your hand.

It's Time to Eat Jelly Beans

Guess the flavor, take a fun bite,

Every jelly bean is a yummy delight.

Some are fruity, and some taste wild,

Each one brings a giggle or smile.

Count them up or sort by hue,

Make patterns of red, green, and blue.

It's not just candy, it's a playful game,

Every jelly bean feels like fame.

Tuck them in pockets or save them for later,

A tiny treasure, like no other flavor.

In a bowl or a jar, they twinkle and shine,

Jelly beans are simply divine.

The joy they bring is easy to see,

Jelly beans make us happy as can be.

It's Time to Eat Jelly Beans

Snack time is better with these little gems,

A sweet little world inside each of them.

So let's all cheer, it's jelly bean time,

A rhyme for a treat so perfectly prime.

Pick your favorite, red, blue, or green,

Nothing's as fun as a jelly bean scene!

Eat them slowly or gobble up fast,

The jelly bean joy is sure to last.

With every chew, there's a flavor surprise,

It's Time to Eat

Jelly Beans

A tiny burst of magic in every size!

ABOUT THE CREATOR

Walter the Educator is one of the pseudonyms for Walter Anderson. Formally educated in Chemistry, Business, and Education, he is an educator, an author, a diverse entrepreneur, and he is the son of a disabled war veteran. "Walter the Educator" shares his time between educating and creating. He holds interests and owns several creative projects that entertain, enlighten, enhance, and educate, hoping to inspire and motivate you. Follow, find new works, and stay up to date with Walter the Educator™ at WaltertheEducator.com

www.ingramcontent.com/pod-product-compliance
Lightning Source LLC
LaVergne TN
LVHW052012060526
838201LV00059B/4001